# SHAKE IT UP!
## Songbook

Gospel Light

## HOW TO MAKE CLEAN COPIES FROM THIS BOOK

### You may make copies of portions of this book with a clean conscience if

- you (or someone in your organization) are the original purchaser;
- you are using the copies you make for a noncommercial purpose (such as teaching or promoting your ministry) within your church or organization;
- you follow the instructions provided in this book.

### However, it is ILLEGAL for you to make copies if

- you are using the material to promote, advertise or sell a product or service other than for ministry fund-raising;
- you are using the material in or on a product for sale; or
- you or your organization are not the original purchaser of this book.

By following these guidelines you help us keep our products affordable.

Thank you,

*Gospel Light*

Editorial Staff
**Publisher,** William T. Greig
**Senior Consulting Publisher,**
Dr. Elmer L. Towns
**Publisher, Research,**
**Planning and Development,**
Billie Baptiste
**Managing Editor,**
Lynnette Pennings, M.A.
**Senior Consulting Editor,**
Wesley Haystead, M.S.Ed.
**Senior Editor,**
**Biblical and Theological Issues,**
Bayard Taylor, M.Div.
**Senior Advisor,**
**Biblical and Theological Issues**,
Dr. Gary S. Greig
**Senior Editor,**
Sheryl Haystead
**Special Products Editor,**
Mary Gross
**Contributing Editors,**
Neva and Anthony Felino,
Gary Pailer, Marc and Judy Roth,
Jay Bea Summerfield
**Senior Designer,**
Carolyn Thomas
**Music Engraver,**
David West

# Table of Contents

# Introduction

### Little children are eager to sing!

They are full of a simple joy that makes them see the world as a wondrous place. That joy often causes them to hum, sing and dance spontaneously. For those of us who love to teach young children, that's good news! No matter if our voices crack or we can't remember all the words—little ones are with us all the way when we begin singing!

**Best of all,** there is probably no more powerful way to implant God's Word and its principles in young children than to sing with them! Think back to the earliest songs you can recall. Did a song often comfort you? Instruct you? Give you a way to express your joy? Songs learned early in life retain significance, and simple songs can plant truth deeply in young hearts where it can grow strong.

**Our children often hear** musical messages that may be contrary to biblical truth. But the songs in this book are a powerful way to combat such messages. These songs communicate God's love and His work in our lives in words a young child can understand. The songs use tunes, rhythms and actions that involve a child's whole self and help a child remember well what God's Word says.

**One warning, however:** grownups will find that the simple truths in these songs bring us back time and again to childlike joy! After all, Jesus invited us to become as little children. He wants us to experience the joy that comes from true security in fully trusting Him as our little ones trust us. As a result, we'll see wonder in every circumstance around us, a wonder that puts a song in our hearts and praise on our lips—very much like what we see in our humming, singing and dancing little ones!

## Using This Book

This songbook has built-in features to help you and your young ones learn and enjoy this new music.

### • Word Charts

Each song in this book has a reproducible word chart. Photocopy the charts you need and post them where you can see them easily to help you stay on track with the songs while you maintain eye contact with children.

Words in **bold type** on the word charts are spoken. Words in (parentheses) are sung echoes or responses. Words in *(italics and parentheses)* are instructions. The choruses of songs are also set in **bold type**.

### • Accompaniments and Chords

Each song offers a simple keyboard arrangement and guitar chords for accompaniment.

### • Reproducible Cassettes and CDs

Every song in this book can be found on the *Shake It Up!* cassettes and *Shake It Up!* CDs.

You may reproduce this music onto cassettes for all the children in your group to aid learning and to build up home libraries of appealing, biblically based music.

*Shake It Up!* cassettes contain reproducible stereo mixes of each song.

*Shake It Up!* CDs contain stereo-mix, reproducible tracks for each song as well as split tracks of the songs for use as an accompaniment.

# All I Need

*Words and Music by Mary Gross*

Food to eat! (Food to eat!) Wa-ter to drink! (Wa-ter to drink!) A house to live in! (A house to live in!) Peo-ple to love me! (Peo-ple to love me!) God cares for me that's all I need!

# All I Need

Food to eat! **Food to eat!**

"food to eat"

Water to drink! **Water to drink!**

A house to live in! **A house to live in!**

"a house to live in"

People to love me! **People to love me!**

God cares for me—that's all I need!

"people to love me"

# God Cares About You

## (1 Peter 5:7)

Words and Music by Mary Gross

God cares a - bout you. (God cares a - bout you.) God cares a - bout

you. (God cares a - bout you.) Em - i - ly, Josh and Britt, God cares a - bout

**1.** you. (God cares a - bout you.) God cares a - bout

**2.** you. (God cares a - bout you.)

Look all a - round. Who's next to you?

# God Cares About You

**(1 Peter 5:7)**

God cares about you. (God cares about you.)
God cares about you. (God cares about you.)
<u>Emily</u>, <u>Josh</u> and <u>Britt</u>,
God cares about you. (God cares about you.)

*Repeat verse, using other names in place of those underlined*

*Chorus:*

**Look all around.** *(Swivel head.)*
**Who's next to you?** *(Look left and then look right.)*
**Tell that friend,** *(Point in both directions.)*
**"God cares about you."**

*Spoken:*

**God cares about you.**
  *(Say to a neighbor.)*
**God cares about you.**
  *(Say to a neighbor.)*
**God cares about who?**
**God cares about you!**
**And you and you and you!**

*Repeat verse, using other names in place of those underlined*

Words and Music by Mary Gross. © 2001 Gospel Light. Permission to photocopy granted. *Shake It Up!*

# A Little Bit More

Words and Music by Neva and Anthony Felino

oth-ers;        It    makes   me   shout,  Hur - ray! "Hur - ray!"

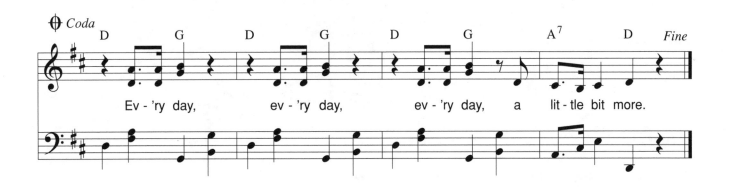

*Coda*

Ev - 'ry day,        ev - 'ry day,        ev - 'ry day,    a    lit - tle bit more.

# A Little Bit More

Every day, I'm growing up
A little bit more,
  a little bit more.
  *(Move hand upward.)*
Every day, I do what's right,
A little bit more,
  a little bit more.
  *(Move hands apart.)*

*Chorus:*

**My ears hear His word;** *(Point to ears.)*

**My eyes see the world He made;** *(Point to eyes.)*

**My hands help others;** *(Hold up hands.)*

**It makes me shout, "Hurray!"**

*Spoken:*

**Hurray!**

*Repeat verse*

Every day, every day, every day, a little bit more.

Action Option: Children squat, stand and stretch to indicate "a little bit more."

# I Love the Lord

## (Psalm 116:1)

Words and Music by Neva and Anthony Felino

# I Love the Lord

**(Psalm 116:1)**

I love the Lord. I love the Lord.

I love the Lord!

<u>Marley</u> says, "I love the Lord."

   *(Point to child named.)*

"when the sun is shining"

When the sun is shining, I love the Lord.

When the rain is falling, I love the Lord.

   *(Make rain fingers.)*

When the wind is blowing, I love the Lord.

<u>Dana</u> says, "I love the Lord."

   *(Point to child.)*

I love the Lord. I love the Lord.

I love the Lord!

<u>Levi</u> says, "I love the Lord."

   *(Point to child named.)*

"when the wind is blowing"

Enrichment Option: Repeat song, using other names for underlined ones.

*Words and Music by Neva and Anthony Felino. © 2001 Gospel Light. Permission to photocopy granted. Shake It Up!*

# What Are You Gonna Do?

Words and Music by Neva and Anthony Felino

show God's love to my <u>mom</u> to-day, Smil - ing while I
"I can show God's. <u>love</u> to-day. Here's a hug for

help! show God's love to - day!___
you!"

# What Are You Gonna Do?

**Chorus:**

**What are you gonna do today?**
**Gonna show God's love in a special way.**
**What are you gonna do today?**
**Gonna show God's love today.**

Gonna show God's love to my <u>mom</u> today;
Gonna help clean up before I play;
  *(Pretend to pick up toys.)*
Gonna show God's love to my <u>mom</u> today,
Smiling while I help!

**Repeat chorus**

Gonna show God's love to my <u>dad</u> today;
Gonna hug my <u>dad</u> and here's what
  I'll say, *(Pretend to hug.)*
"I can show God's love today.
  Here's a hug for you!"

**Repeat chorus**

Action Option: While singing chorus,
shrug shoulders and then hug self.

Enrichment Options:
1. Insert other titles (teacher,
   aunt, etc.) for underlined ones.

2. Repeat song, making up additional verses such as:
   Friend/Gonna share my toys when we play today/I can share my toys.
   Pet/Gonna feed my per every day/I can help my pet!

Words and Music by Neva and Anthony Felino. © 2001 Gospel Light. Permission to photocopy granted. *Shake It Up!*

# With Love

## (Galatians 5:13)

*Words and Music by Mary Gross*

With love! With love! Help each oth - er. With

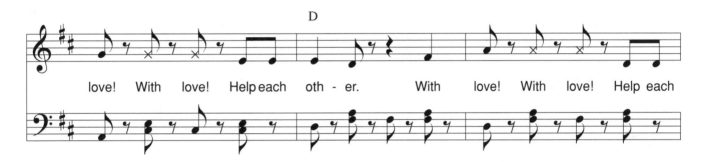

love! With love! Help each oth - er. With love! With love! Help each

**1.** oth - er. This is what God says. With

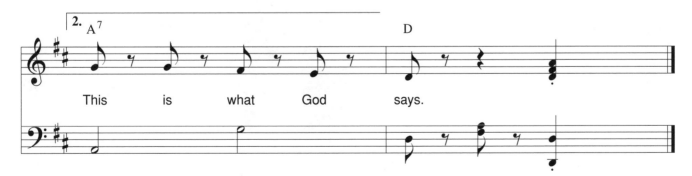

**2.** This is what God says.

**Spoken:**
**Stand up tall! Take a breath. March your feet and sing!**

# With Love

**(Galatians 5:13)**

With love! **With love!**

Help each other.

With love! **With love!**

Help each other.

With love! **With love!**

Help each other.

This is what God says.

*Spoken:*

**Stand up tall!**

**Take a breath.**

**March your feet**

**And sing!**

*Repeat song*

"march your feet"

# Good News

Words and Music by Neva and Anthony Felino

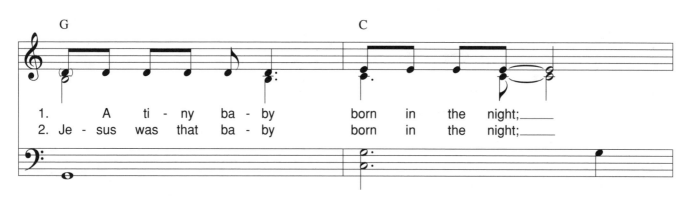

1. A ti - ny ba - by    born    in    the    night;____
2. Je - sus was that ba - by    born    in    the    night;____

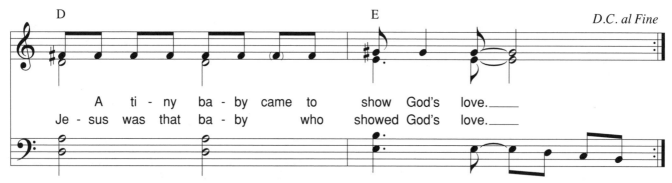

*D.C. al Fine*

A    ti - ny ba - by came to    show God's love.____
Je - sus was that ba - by    who    showed God's love.____

# Good News

*Chorus:*

**Good news, <u>children</u>!**

  **Yes, I've got good news.**

**Good news, <u>children</u>!**

  **Yes, I've got good news.**

**Good news, <u>children</u>!**

  **Yes, I've got good news.**

**Good news, <u>children</u>!**

  **Yes, I've got good news.**

"good news"

"tiny baby"

1. A tiny baby born in the night,

   A tiny baby came to show God's love.

*Chorus*

2. Jesus was that baby born in the night; *(Nod.)*

   Jesus was that baby who showed God's love.

*Chorus*

Enrichment Option: Insert different children's names or "mommies/daddies/brothers/sisters" in place of "children."

# God Loved Us

## (1 John 4:10)

Words and Music by Neva and Anthony Felino

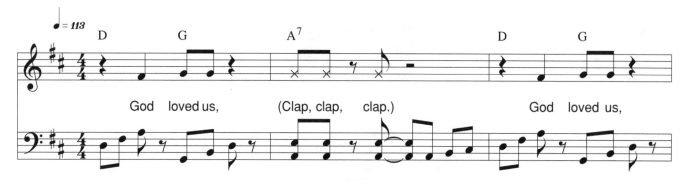

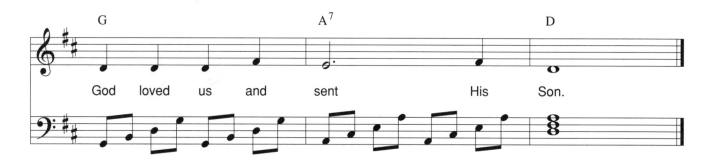

**Spoken:**
(Give one instruction before each repetition of song.)
**Very softly.**
**A little louder.**
**Even louder!**

# God Loved Us

**(1 John 4:10)**

God loved us, *(Clap three times.)*

God loved us, *(Clap three times.)*

God loved us, *(Clap three times.)*

God loved us and sent His Son.

*Spoken:*

*(Give one instruction before
 each repetition of song.)*

**Very softly.**

**A little louder.**

**Even louder!**

**Repeat song three more times**

Action Option: Vary clapping pattern.

# Every Day

Words and Music by Neva and Anthony Felino

1. Je - sus loves me ev - 'ry day,___ ev - 'ry day,___
2. Je - sus helps me ev - 'ry day,___ ev - 'ry day,___

ev - 'ry day;___ Je - sus loves me ev - 'ry day___ and
ev - 'ry day;___ Je - sus helps me ev - 'ry day___ and

I'm so glad He does!___ I know Je - sus loves___ me
I'm so glad He does!___

Ev - en when I'm sad.___ I know He will help___ me;

That al - ways makes me glad! I'm so glad He does!___

# Every Day

Jesus loves me every day,

every day, every day;

*(Wave arms and wiggle fingers.)*

Jesus loves me every day

and I'm so glad He does!

Jesus helps me every day,

every day, every day;

*(Wave arms and wiggle fingers.)*

Jesus helps me every day

and I'm so glad He does!

I know Jesus loves me *(Hug self.)*

Even when I'm <u>sad</u>.

I know He will help me;

That always makes me glad! *(Clap.)*

Jesus helps me every day, every day, every day;

*(Wave arms and wiggle fingers.)*

Jesus helps me every day and I'm so glad He does!

Enrichment Option: Insert a word describing an emotion
    ("glad," "scared," "mad," "tired," etc.) for underlined word.

*Words and Music by Neva and Anthony Felino. © 2001 Gospel Light. Permission to photocopy granted. Shake It Up!*

# I Will Sing

## (Psalm 89:1)

Words and Music by Neva and Anthony Felino

When I'm splash-ing in my bath, I will sing,

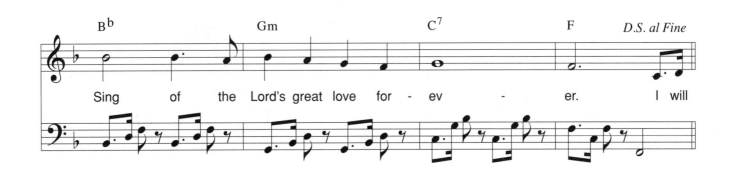

Sing of the Lord's great love for - ev - er. I will

29

# I Will Sing

**(Psalm 89:1)**

I will sing, I will sing, I will sing

Of the Lord's great love forever.

*(Stretch arms out to sides.)*

I will sing, I will sing, I will sing

Of the Lord's great love forever.

*(Stretch arms out to sides.)*

When I'm <u>walking down the street</u>, I will sing.

When I'm <u>riding in the car</u>, I will sing.

When I'm <u>splashing in my bath</u>, I will sing,

Sing of the Lord's great love forever.

*(Stretch arms out to sides.)*

I will sing, I will sing, I will sing

Of the Lord's great love forever.

*(Stretch arms out to sides.)*

I will sing, I will sing, I will sing

Of the Lord's great love forever.

*(Stretch arms out to sides.)*

"walking down
the street"

"riding in
the car"

"splashing
in my
bath"

Action Option: Insert "jumping up and down/bending to the ground/swaying back and forth" for underlined words.

Enrichment Option: Insert "swinging in the swing/playing with my toys/lying in my bed" for underlined words.

*Words and Music by Neva and Anthony Felino. © 2001 Gospel Light. Permission to photocopy granted. Shake It Up!*

# Help Me Be Kind

Words and Music by Neva and Anthony Felino

1. When it is morn-ing time, help me be kind,
2. When it is night - time, help me be kind,

Help me be kind, help me be kind. When it is morn-ing time,
Help me be kind, help me be kind. When it is night - time,

help me be kind, just like Je - sus was.
help me be kind, just like Je - sus was.

When it's time to get up, I'll rise with a smile; That is a way
When it's time for bed, I will get ready; I'll brush my teeth;

# Help Me Be Kind

When it is <u>morning time</u>, help me be kind,
Help me be kind, help me be kind.
When it is <u>morning time</u>, help me be kind,
  just like Jesus was.
When it's time to get up, I'll rise with
  a smile; *(Pretend to yawn and stretch.)*
That is a way I can be kind!
When it's time to get dressed,
  I'll do my best; *(Pretend to dress.)*
"Lord, help me be kind today."

"rise with a smile"

When it is <u>nighttime</u>, help me be kind,
Help me be kind, help me be kind.
When it is <u>nighttime</u>, help me be kind,
  just like Jesus was.
When it's time for bed, I will get ready;
I'll brush my teeth; I'll get my teddy.
  *(Pretend to brush teeth.)*
When I hop into bed, here's what
  I'll say: *(Pretend to pull up covers.)*
"God helped me be kind today!"

"brush my teeth"

Action Option: Gently pat a neighbor's shoulder as you sing "Help me be kind."

Enrichment Option: Insert "daytime," "breakfast time," "playtime," "lunchtime" or "nap time" for underlined words.

*Words and Music by Neva and Anthony Felino. © 2001 Gospel Light. Permission to photocopy granted. Shake It Up!*

# Be Kind

## (2 Timothy 2:24)

Words and Music by Bernice Marlo

Be kind, be kind to ev-'ry-one. Be kind, be kind to ev-'ry-one. Be

kind, be kind to ev'-ry-one. The Bi-ble says, "Be kind."

*2x Fine*

Skip to a friend, skip back to your place.

Turn a-round, put a smile on your face, And sing with me, "Be kind." Be

*D.C. al Fine*

# Be Kind

**(2 Timothy 2:24)**

*Chorus:*

**Be kind, be kind to everyone.**

**Be kind, be kind to everyone.**

**Be kind, be kind to everyone.**

**The Bible says, "Be kind."**

Skip to a friend, skip back to your place.

*(Children skip as music plays.)*

Turn around, put a smile on your face,

And sing with me, "Be kind."

*Chorus*

# Jesus Is Alive!

Words and Music by Neva and Anthony Felino.

1. I am hap-py and I'll tell you why:___ Je-sus is a-live!___ I am hap-py and I'll tell you why:___
2. Ma-ry was hap-py and I'll tell you why:___ Je-sus is a-live!___ Chad is hap-py and he'll tell you why:___
3. We are hap-py and we'll tell you why:___ Je-sus is a-live!___ We are hap-py and we'll tell you why:___

Je-sus is a-live!___ Well, it makes me want to sing and it makes me want to shout;

*3x to Coda*

I've got some-thing to be hap-py a-bout!___

Coda

Je - sus is a - live!_____ Je - sus is a - live!___

___ Je - sus is a - live!_____

# Jesus Is Alive!

I am happy and I'll tell you why:
   Jesus is alive! *(Squat and then stand.)*
I am happy and I'll tell you why:
   Jesus is alive! *(Squat and then stand.)*

Well, it makes me want to sing and it makes me want to shout;
I've got something to be happy about!

Mary was happy and I'll tell you why: Jesus is alive!
   *(Squat and then stand.)*
Chad is happy and he'll tell you why: Jesus is alive!
   *(Squat and then stand.)*

Well, it makes me want to sing and it makes me want to shout;
I've got something to be happy about!

We are happy and we'll tell you why:
   Jesus is alive! *(Squat and then stand.)*
We are happy and we'll tell you why:
   Jesus is alive! *(Squat and then stand.)*
Jesus is alive! Jesus is alive!

**Action Option:** Clap during chorus and then give
each other high fives at the end of the chorus.

# Sing Praises
## (Psalm 9:11)

Words and Music by Neva and Anthony Felino

Sing, sing; Sing, oh sing,

Sing praises to the Lord.

**2.** Lord. Clap your hands and sing, sing, sing;___

Wave your arms and sing, sing, sing;___ Snap your fin-gers, Sing

praises to the Lord. Lord.

# Sing Praises

**(Psalm 9:11)**

*Chorus:*

*(Raise hands and wiggle fingers as "la, la, la, la" is sung.)*

**Sing (la, la, la, la), sing (la, la, la, la);**

**Sing, oh sing (la, la, la, la),**

**Sing (la, la, la, la) praises to the Lord (la, la, la, la).**

*Repeat chorus*

Clap your hands and sing, sing, sing;

Wave your arms and sing, sing, sing;

<u>Snap your fingers</u>,

Sing praises to the Lord.

*Repeat chorus*

Action option: Insert "stomp your feet" or "nod your head"
for underlined words, especially when singing with younger children.

# Who Needs Help?

Words and Music by Neva and Anthony Felino.

Who___ needs help? I look and see___ Some-one to help right next to me. I can help, I can share, Tell a-bout Je-sus, An-y- time, an - y - where.___ right next to me.

# Who Needs Help?

Who needs help? I look and see
  *(Shade eyes and look side to side.)*
Someone to help right next to me.
  *(Point to neighbor.)*

Who needs help? I look and see
  *(Shade eyes and look side to side.)*
Someone to help right next to me.
  *(Point to neighbor.)*

I can help, I can share,
Tell about Jesus,
Anytime, anywhere.

Who needs help? I look and see
  *(Shade eyes and look side to side.)*
Someone to help right next to me.
  *(Point to neighbor.)*

# Hear the Word

## (Luke 11:28)

Words and Music by Neva and Anthony Felino

Hear the word, hear the word, Hear the word of God and o-

bey it. Hear the word, hear the word,

Hear the word of God and o-bey it. *March in place, hear the word!*

*Back and forth, hear the word!*

*Turn a-round.* Hear the word of God and o-bey it.

# Hear the Word

**(Luke 11:28)**

Hear the word, hear the word,

Hear the word of God and obey it.

 *(Nod while singing "obey.")*

Hear the word, hear the word,

Hear the word of God and obey it.

"hear"

"back and forth"

<u>March in place</u>, hear the word! *(March in place.)*

<u>Back and forth</u>, hear the word!

<u>Turn around</u>. *(Clap three times while turning.)*

Hear the word of God and obey it.

Hear the word, hear the word,

Hear the word of God and obey it.

Hear the word, hear the word,

Hear the word of God and obey it.

"turn around"

**Action Option:** Insert "Give a smile/Shake a hand/ Pat a back" or "Clap your hands/Stomp your feet/Take a bow" for underlined words.

Words and Music by Neva and Anthony Felino. © 2001 Gospel Light. Permission to photocopy granted. *Shake It Up!*

# In a Very Big Way

Words and Music by Neva and Anthony Felino

Nah nah nah nah___ nah,___ hi - dey hi - dey hey,___

God loves you___ in a ve - ry big way.___

When you're a - fraid,___ God loves you, hi - dey hey!___

When you're sad,___ in a ve - ry big way,___

When you need help,____ hi - dey, hi - dey hey,____

He'll help you____ in a ve - ry big way.____

*D.C. al Fine*

# In a Very Big Way

Nah nah nah nah nah, hidey hidey hey,

God loves you in a very big way. *(Stretch arms out to sides.)*

Nah nah nah nah nah, hidey hidey hey,

God loves you in a very big way. *(Stretch arms out to sides.)*


When you're afraid, God loves you, hidey hey!

When you're sad, in a very big way,

When you need help, hidey, hidey hey,

He'll help you in a very big way. *(Stretch arms out to sides.)*


Nah nah nah nah nah, hidey hidey hey,

God loves you in a very big way.

 *(Stretch arms out to sides.)*

Nah nah nah nah nah, hidey hidey hey,

God loves you in a very big way.

 *(Stretch arms out to sides.)*

**Action Option: Wave hands while singing "Nah nah nah nah nah."**
**Point and shake finger while singing "Hidey hidey hey."**

# God's Love

## (1 John 3:1)

Words and Music by Neva and Anthony Felino.

# God's Love

**(1 John 3:1)**

*Chorus:*

**God's love (God's love)**

**For us (for us)**

**Is great (is great),**

**Is great (is great);**

**God's love for us is great.**

*Repeat chorus*

Clap your hands (God's love).

Stand on up (God's love).

Stomp your feet (God's love).

Nod your head and sing,

"God's love for us is great."

*Repeat chorus*

Action Option: Challenge children to clap, stomp and nod from the verse through the end of the song.

*Words and Music by Neva and Anthony Felino. © 2001 Gospel Light. Permission to photocopy granted. Shake It Up!*

# My Family

Words and Music: Neva and Anthony Felino

# My Family

I love my family; I want to treat them right.

I'll show I love them, every day and every night.

I'll <u>be kind</u>; <u>I'll forgive</u>.

I'll tell the truth; it's the best way to live!

I love my family;

I want to treat them right.

I'll show I love them,

every day and every night.

Action Option: Hug self each time the word "love" is sung.

Enrichment Option: Insert children's ideas for underlined words.

*Words and Music by Neva and Anthony Felino. © 2001 Gospel Light. Permission to photocopy granted. Shake It Up!*

# Let Us Love

## (1 John 4:7)

Words and Music by Neva and Anthony Felino

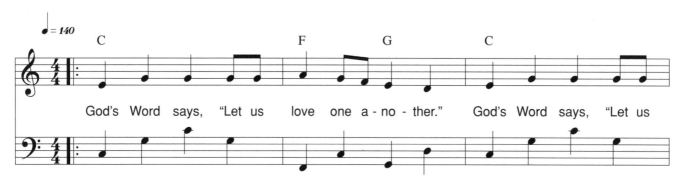

God's Word says, "Let us love one a - no - ther." God's Word says, "Let us

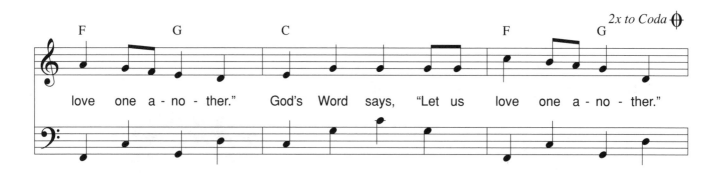

love one a - no - ther." God's Word says, "Let us love one a - no - ther."

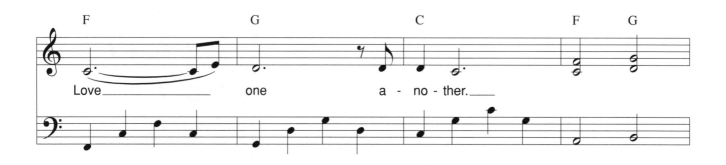

Love_____ one a - no - ther.___

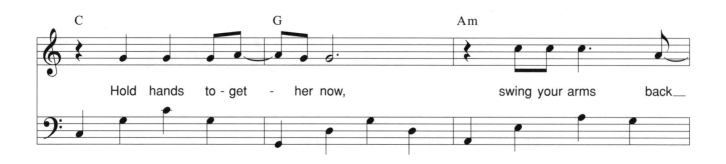

Hold hands to - get - her now, swing your arms back___

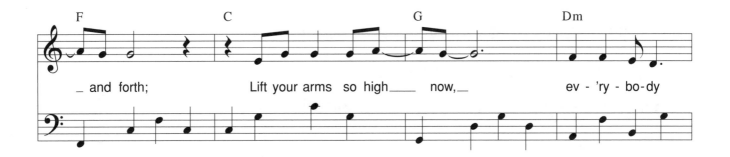

_ and forth;  Lift your arms so high___ now,___  ev - 'ry - bo-dy

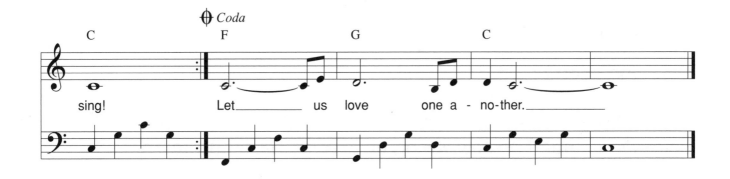

sing!  Let_____ us  love  one a - no-ther._____

# Let Us Love

**(1 John 4:7)**

God's Word says, "Let us love one another."

 *(Hold hand of person on right.)*

God's Word says, "Let us love one another."

 *(Hold hand of person on left.)*

God's Word says, "Let us love one another."

 *(Hold hands and sway.)*

Love one another.


Hold hands together now, swing your arms back and forth;

Lift your arms so high now, everybody sing! *(Pairs raise arms.)*


God's Word says,

 "Let us love one another."

God's Word says,

 "Let us love one another."

God's Word says,

 "Let us love one another."

Let us love one another.

"hold hands together now, swing your arms back and forth"

# I Can Talk to God

Words and Music by Neva and Anthony Felino

1. When I'm out - side play - ing in the yard,____
   When I'm in - side rest - ing on my bed,____
2. When I'm cry - ing be - cause I am sad,____
   When I don't feel__ like do - ing what is right,____

I can talk to God,____ I can talk to God.____
I can talk to God,____ I can talk to God.____
I can talk to God,____ I can talk to God.____
I can talk to God,____ I can talk to God.____

__ I can tell God all a - bout__ my

day; I ask Him to help__ me live His

# I Can Talk to God

When I'm outside <u>playing in the yard</u>,

   I can talk to God, I can talk to God.

When I'm inside <u>resting on my bed</u>,

   I can talk to God, I can talk to God.

"I can talk"  "to God"

I can tell God all about my day;

   I ask Him to help me live His way;

Then "I love You" is what I say,

   'cause I can talk to God anytime.

"anytime"

When I'm crying because I'm sad,

   I can talk to God, I can talk to God.

When I don't feel like doing what's right,

   I can talk to God, I can talk to God.

Oh, I tell God all about my day;

   I ask Him to help me live His way;

Then "I love You" is what I say,

'cause I can talk to God anytime.

   'Cause I can talk to God anytime.

"I love you"

Enrichment Option: Insert children's ideas for underlined words.

Words and Music by Neva and Anthony Felino. © 2001 Gospel Light. Permission to photocopy granted. *Shake It Up!*

# Love the Lord

**(Matthew 22:37)**

Words and Music by Neva and Anthony Felino

# Love the Lord

**(Matthew 22:37)**

Love, love, love (ooooh),
Love the Lord your God.
Love, love, love (ooooh),
Love the Lord your God.

"love"

<u>Tessa</u> and <u>Zachary</u>,
   love the Lord your God.
   *(Point to children named.)*
<u>Katherine</u> and <u>Jared</u>,
   love the Lord your God.
   *(Point to children named.)*
Love, love, love (ooooh),
Love the Lord your God.
Love, love, love (ooooh),
Love the Lord your God.

"love"

"love"

Action Option: Raise hands higher each time
you sing "love," wiggling fingers. Wave hands
in the air each time "ooooh" is sung.

Words and Music by Neva and Anthony Felino. © 2001 Gospel Light. Permission to photocopy granted. *Shake It Up!*

# Helpin' Out

Words and Music by Neva and Anthony Felino

*Reggae feel* ♩ = 134

Help, help, help-in', I'm help-in' out.

Help, help, help-in', I'm help-in' out.

Well, the Bi-ble says___ to

show God's love___ And one way to do it is help-in' out.___ Well, the

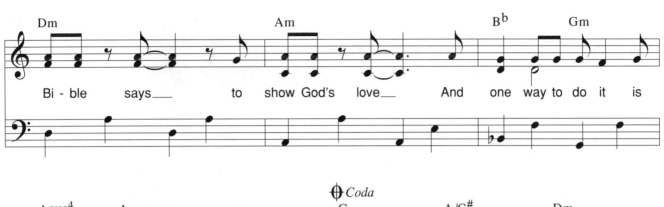

Bi - ble says___ to show God's love___ And one way to do it is

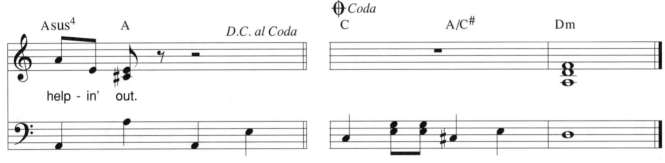

help - in' out.

# Helpin' Out

Help, help, helpin', I'm helpin' out.

Help, help, helpin', I'm helpin' out.

Help, help, helpin', I'm helpin' out.

Help, help, helpin', I'm helpin' out.

Well, the Bible says to show God's love

And one way to do it is helpin' out.

Well, the Bible says to show God's love

And one way to do it is helpin' out.

"help, help"

"helpin'"

Action Option: Pat knees and clap hands while singing "Help, help, helpin'" (see sketches). Point to children who are helping as you sing (see Enrichment Option below).

Enrichment Option: Insert children's names in song. For example:

Nona is helpin', she's helpin' out;

Arvan's helpin', he's helpin' out;

Sophia's helpin', she's helpin' out;

Casey's helpin', he's helpin' out.

*Words and Music by Neva and Anthony Felino. © 2001 Gospel Light. Permission to photocopy granted. Shake It Up!*

# Love Is

## (1 Corinthians 13:4)

Words and Music by Neva and Anthony Felino

# Love Is

**(1 Corinthians 13:4)**

"make yourself very small"

God says, "Love is patient,"

God says, "Love is kind."

God says, "Love is patient, love is kind."

God says, "Love is patient,"

God says, "Love is kind."

God says, "Love is patient, love is kind."

Make yourself very small and whisper,

**"Love is patient, love is kind."**

"stand up and clap your hands"

Stand up and clap your hands and say it,

**"Love is patient, love is kind."**

Reach up to the sky and shout it,

"Love is patient, love is kind!"

"reach up to the sky"

**Repeat song**

Words and Music by Neva and Anthony Felino. © 2001 Gospel Light. Permission to photocopy granted. *Shake It Up!*

# God Made the World

Words and Music by Marc and Judy Roth

God made the world and ev-'ry-thing in it, God made the land and the sky and sea;___ God made fish and the wa-ter they swim in, God made the world and God made me! God made flo-wers; God made bees. God made birds___ and God

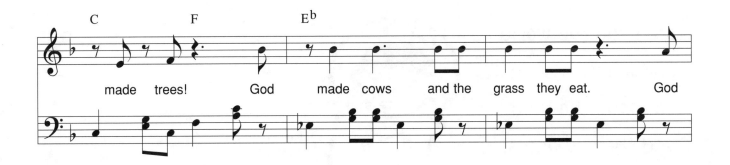

made trees! God made cows and the grass they eat. God

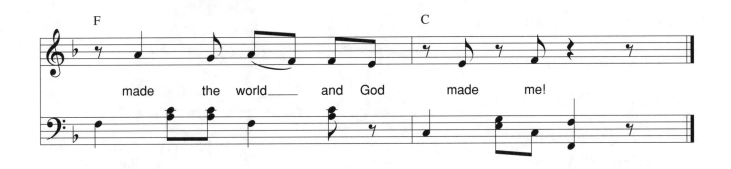

made the world____ and God made me!

# God Made the World

God made the world
and everything in it,
God made the land
and the sky and sea;
God made fish and the
water they swim in,
God made the world
and God made me!
*(Make world and
then point to self.)*

God made flowers;
God made bees.
God made birds and
God made trees!
God made cows and
the grass they eat.
God made the world
and God made me!

"the world"

"sea,"
"water"

"fish"

"cows"

Action Option: Pretend to be the animals named.

*Words and Music by Marc and Judy Roth. © 2001 Gospel Light. Permission to photocopy granted. Shake It Up!*

# God Made

## (Acts 17:24)

Traditional Music

# God Made

**(Acts 17:24)**

God made the world

And everything in it.

God made the world

And everything in it.

**Spoken:**

**Hear the chime? What's the time?**

**Count the hours with me!**

*(Take one step for each sound of the chime. Count chime repetitions aloud, counting on fingers.)*

God made the world

And everything in it.

God made the world

And everything in it.

Everything in it.

# God Helps Me Do Good Things

Words and Music by Marc and Judy Roth

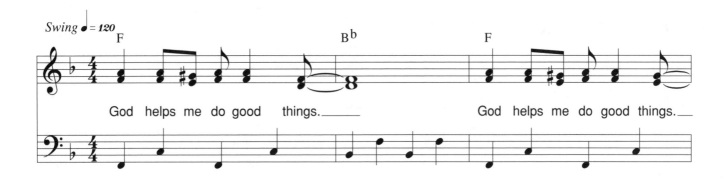

God helps me do good things._____ God helps me do good things.__

__ Ev - 'ry day I can do my best, be - cause

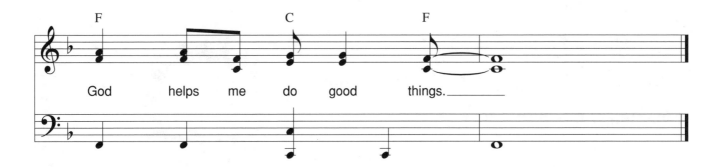

God helps me do good things._____

**Spoken:**
*(Repeat question to several children, using their names in place of underlined name. Each child responds.)*
**What's a good thing you can do, <u>Marya</u>?**

# God Helps Me Do Good Things

God helps me do good things.

God helps me do good things.

Every day I can <u>do my best</u>, because

God helps me do good things.


***Spoken:***

*(Repeat question to several children, using their names*

*in place of underlined name. Each child responds.)*

**What's a good thing you can do, <u>Marya</u>?**


God helps me do good things.

God helps me do good things.

Every day I can <u>thank the Lord</u>, because

God helps me do good things.

Action Option: Pound fists while singing
"God helps me do good things."

Enrichment Option: Insert "sing to God,"
"help my mom," "give God praise" or
children's ideas for underlined words.

*Words and Music by Marc and Judy Roth. © 2001 Gospel Light. Permission to photocopy granted. Shake It Up!*

# Do Good

## (Ephesians 2:10)

Words and Music by Mary Gross

God made___ us to do good, God made___ us to do good,

God made___ us to do good, God made us to do good.

**Spoken:**

**Clap high! God made** *(Clap twice.)*

**Clap low! God made** *(Clap twice.)*

**Clap side to side! God made us to do good.**

*(Clap three times.)*

# Do Good

**(Ephesians 2:10)**

God made us to do good, *(Clap.)*

God made us to do good, *(Clap.)*

God made us to do good, *(Clap.)*

God made us to do good.

*Spoken:*

**Clap high! God made** *(Clap twice.)*

**Clap low! God made** *(Clap twice.)*

**Clap side to side! God made us to do good.**

*(Clap three times.)*

God made us to do good, *(Clap.)*

God made us to do good, *(Clap.)*

God made us to do good, *(Clap.)*

God made us to do good.

Action Option: To challenge older children, increase the number of claps or vary the clapping pattern at the end of each line.

*Words and Music by Mary Gross.* © 2001 Gospel Light. Permission to photocopy granted. *Shake It Up!*

# Choosing Song

Words and Music by Mary Gross

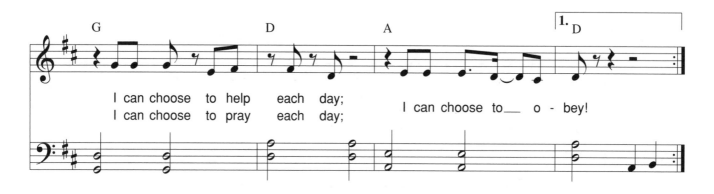

I can choose to help each day;
I can choose to pray each day;
I can choose to\_ o - bey!

bey!
I can choose to\_ o - bey!

# Choosing Song

Sometimes I get to choose what I eat; *(Pretend to eat.)*

Sometimes I choose the shoes for my feet. *(Point to shoes.)*

Sometimes I try to pour my own juice, *(Pretend to pour.)*

But here are things I can always choose: *(Hold up two fingers.)*

I can choose to help each day;
  I can choose to obey! *(Count on fingers.)*
I can choose to help each day;
  I can choose to obey! *(Count on fingers.)*

Some days I get to choose what to wear;
  *(Pretend to put on jacket.)*

Some days I choose to brush my hair.
  *(Pretend to brush hair.)*

Some days I try to tie my own shoes,
  *(Pretend to tie.)*

But here are things I can always choose:
  *(Hold up two fingers.)*

I can choose to pray each day; I can choose to obey!
  *(Count on fingers.)*

I can choose to pray each day; I can choose to obey!
  *(Count on fingers.)*

I can choose to obey!

*Words and Music by Mary Gross. © 2001 Gospel Light. Permission to photocopy granted. Shake It Up!*

# Obey the Lord

## (Deuteronomy 27:10)

Words and Music by Marc and Judy Roth

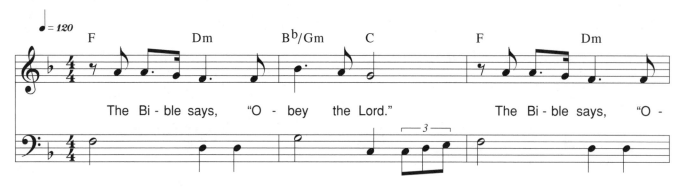

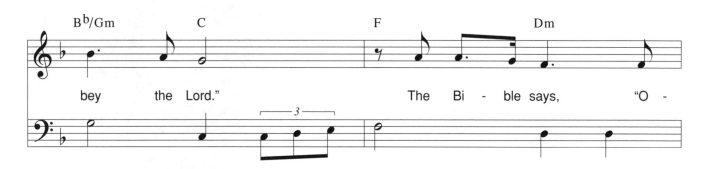

The Bi - ble says, "O - bey the Lord." The Bi - ble says, "O - bey the Lord." The Bi - ble says, "O -

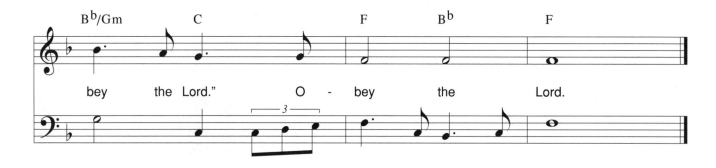

bey the Lord." O - bey the Lord.

**Spoken:**
**O-** *(Step right.)*
**-bey** *(Step left.)*
**the** *(Step right.)*
**Lord.** *(Step left.)*

# Obey the Lord

**(Deuteronomy 27:10)**

The Bible says, "Obey the Lord."

The Bible says, "Obey the Lord."

The Bible says, "Obey the Lord."

Obey the Lord.

**Spoken:**

**O-** *(Step right.)*

**-bey** *(Step left.)*

**the** *(Step right.)*

**Lord.** *(Step left.)*

**Repeat step sequence**

Pretend
to play
drums.

Action Option: Snap fingers or pretend to play instruments (guitar, trumpet, drum, etc.).

Words and Music by Marc and Judy Roth. © 2001 Gospel Light. Permission to photocopy granted. *Shake It Up!*

# The Angels Sing

Words and Music by Debbie Barber and Mary Gross

# The Angels Sing

The angels sing (la, la, la);
The shepherds laugh (**ha, ha, ha**).
The donkey brays (**hee-haw, hee-haw**);
The crows all caw (**caw, caw, caw**).

"Moo-oo," lows the cow (moooooo);
"Bah-bahh," says the sheep (baaaaaah).
Mary smiles

***Spoken:***
**Give a great big smile!** *(Smile.)*

And Joseph leaps.

***Spoken:***
**Leap your fingers!** *(Leap fingers.)*

"Moo-oo," lows the cow (moooooo);
"Bah-bahh," says the sheep (baaaaaah).
How on earth can God's baby sleep?
  *(Shrug shoulders.)*
How on earth can God's baby sleep?

# God's Son

## (Isaiah 9:6)

Words and Music by Marc and Judy Roth

God's Son (God's Son) Is born for us (is born for us);

God's Son (God's Son) Is born for us (is born for us);

God's Son (God's Son) Is born for us (is born for us);

God's Son is born for us.

**Spoken:**

(*March during spoken portion. Teacher asks questions; children answer.*)

**Whose Son is born? God's Son, Jesus!**

**He's born for whom? He's born for us!**

# God's Son
## (Isaiah 9:6)

God's Son (God's Son)

Is born for us (is born for us);

God's Son (God's Son)

Is born for us (is born for us);

God's Son (God's Son)

Is born for us (is born for us);

God's Son is born for us.

### *Spoken:*

*(March during spoken portion.
Teacher asks questions;
children answer.)*

**Whose Son is born?**

  **God's Son, Jesus!**

**He's born for whom?**

  **He's born for us!**

### *Repeat song*

# Jesus

Words and Music by Gary Pailer

1. Je - sus, You're God's on - ly Son.

Je - sus, You love me and ev - 'ry - one;

Je - sus, I'm pre - cious to You. I

want You to know, Je - sus, I love You, too.

# Jesus

Jesus, You're God's only Son.

Jesus, You love me

  and everyone;

"Jesus"

Jesus, I'm precious to You.

I want You to know,

Jesus, I love You, too.

"I love you"

# God So Loved

## (John 3:16)

Words and Music by Mary Gross and Karen McGraw

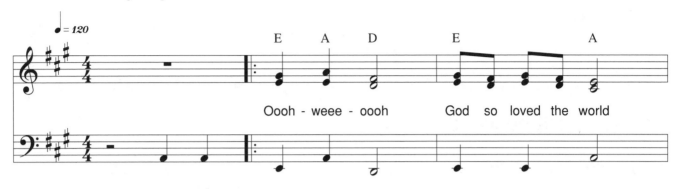

Oooh - weee - oooh    God so loved the world

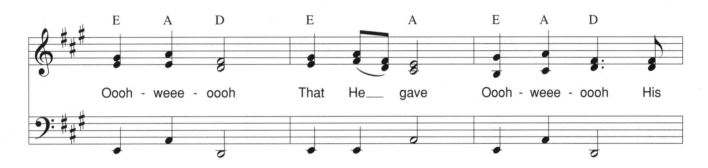

Oooh - weee - oooh    That He___ gave    Oooh - weee - oooh    His

one and on - ly Son    Oooh - weee - oooh    God so loved the world.

# God So Loved
**(John 3:16)**

Oooh-weee-oooh *(Raise hands, turn around and wiggle fingers.)*

God so loved the world

Oooh-weee-oooh *(Raise hands, turn around and wiggle fingers.)*

That He gave

Oooh-weee-oooh *(Raise hands, turn around and wiggle fingers.)*

His one and only Son

Oooh-weee-oooh *(Raise hands, turn around and wiggle fingers.)*

God so loved the world.

**Repeat**

Enrichment Option:
Divide class into two
groups—one group
sings "Oooh-weee-oooh"
and the other group
sings the words; groups
trade assignments when
the song is repeated.

# Jesus Loves You and Me

*Words and Music by Marc and Judy Roth*

He loves you, He loves me; He loves ev - 'ry child He sees.

Je - sus lis - tens when we pray;

He'll take care of us___ ev - 'ry day.

# Jesus Loves You and Me

He loves you, He loves me;

  *(Point to neighbor and then to self.)*

He loves every child He sees.

  *(Point at several others.)*

Jesus listens when we pray;

  *(Cup hand behind ear.)*

He'll take care of us every day.

  *(Hug self.)*

**Repeat song**

# I Will Be Glad

**(Psalm 31:7)**

Words and Music by Marc and Judy Roth

I will be glad, ___ I will be glad, ___ I will be glad ___ and re-joice ___ in Your love. I will be glad, ___ I will be glad, ___ And re-joice ___ in Your love. I will (I will) Be glad (be glad) And re-joice (and re-joice) In Your love (in Your love). I will (I will) Be glad (be glad) And re-joice (and re-joice) In Your love (in Your love).

# I Will Be Glad

**(Psalm 31:7)**

I will be glad, I will be glad,

I will be glad and rejoice in Your love.

I will be glad, I will be glad,

And rejoice in Your love.

I will (I will) *(Point to self.)*

Be glad (be glad) *(Pat chest.)*

And rejoice (and rejoice)

  *(Clap hands over head.)*

In Your love (in Your love). *(Hug self.)*

**Repeat song**

# What Does Jesus Teach?

Words and Music by Marc and Judy Roth

What does Je-sus teach us to do?__ Count them, four or three or two:__ One, be kind. Two, please share.__ Three, give thanks. Four, do good ev - 'ry - where.__

# What Does Jesus Teach?

What does Jesus teach us to do?

Count them, four or three or two: *(Count on fingers.)*

<u>One</u>, be kind. <u>Two</u>, please share.

<u>Three</u>, give thanks. <u>Four</u>, do good everywhere.

Action Option: Children also demonstrate the sign for "Jesus."

Enrichment Option: Insert children's names in place of underlined words, pointing at each child as he or she is named.

"Jesus"

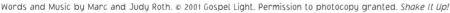

# Give Thanks

## (1 Chronicles 16:34)

Words and Music by Marc and Judy Roth

Give thanks (clap, clap) To the Lord, (clap, clap) His

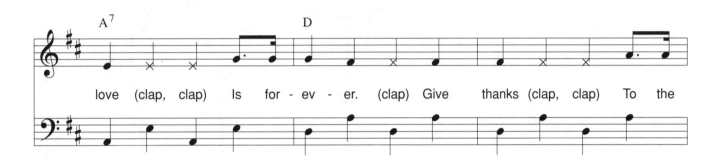

love (clap, clap) Is for - ev - er. (clap) Give thanks (clap, clap) To the

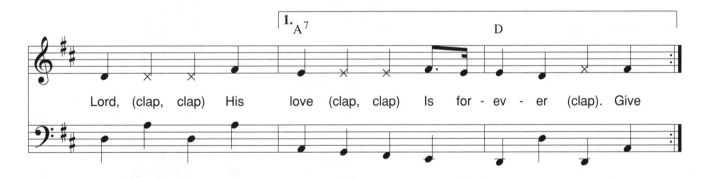

Lord, (clap, clap) His love (clap, clap) Is for - ev - er (clap). Give

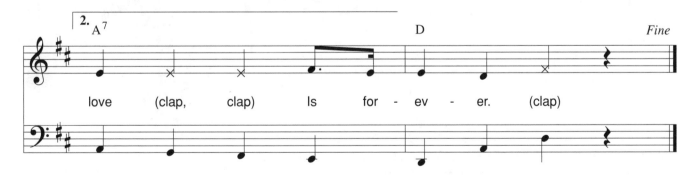

love (clap, clap) Is for - ev - er. (clap)

# Give Thanks

**(1 Chronicles 16:34)**

Give thanks *(Clap twice.)*

To the Lord, *(Clap twice.)*

His love *(Clap twice.)*

Is forever. *(Clap.)*


Give thanks *(Clap twice.)*

To the Lord, *(Clap twice.)*

His love *(Clap twice.)*

Is forever. *(Clap.)*

Action Option: Instead of clapping, stomp or use the motions for "Head and Shoulders, Knees and Toes" (challenge older children to do these actions in reverse order).

*Words and Music by Marc and Judy Roth.* © 2001 Gospel Light. Permission to photocopy granted. *Shake It Up!*

# Praise the Lord

*Words and Music by Mary Gross*

live to - day,___ He is___ a - live.

live.

# Praise the Lord

Praise the Lord, praise the Lord.

Sing alleluia, praise the Lord.

Jesus is risen, He is risen indeed.

Jesus is risen, He is risen indeed.

He is alive, He is alive.

He is alive today, He is alive.

Action Option: Skip or walk in a circle while singing first stanza; move from squatting to standing while singing second stanza; clap over head while singing third stanza.

# How Good It Is

## (Psalm 147:1)

Words and Music by Wes Gorospe and Mary Gross

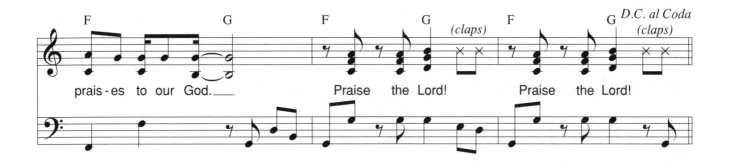

prais - es to our God.___  Praise the Lord! Praise the Lord!

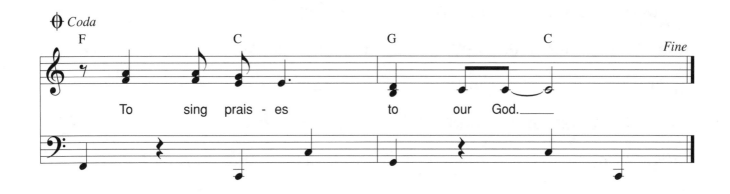

To sing prais - es to our God.___

# How Good It Is

**(Psalm 147:1)**

*Chorus:*

**How good, how good, how good, how good it is**

*(Give a thumbs-up sign.)*

**To sing praises to our God.**

*(Place hands around mouth as if shouting.)*

**How good, how good, how good, how good it is**

*(Give a thumbs-up sign.)*

**To sing praises to our God.**

*(Place hands around mouth as if shouting.)*

How good it is to sing
   praises to our God;
How good it is to sing
   praises to our God.
Praise the Lord!
Praise the Lord!

*Chorus*

# We Can Tell About Jesus

Words and Music by Marc and Judy Roth

♩ = 130

We can tell a - bout Je - sus, We can tell how He loves us; We can

tell a - bout Je - sus, And the great things God has done.

**Spoken:**

*(Repeat question to several children. Each child responds.)*

**What's a great thing God has done?**

# We Can Tell About Jesus

We can tell about Jesus,

We can tell how He loves us;

We can tell about Jesus,

And the great things God has done.

**Spoken:**

*(Repeat question to several children. Each child responds.)*

**What's a great thing God has done?**

We can tell about Jesus,

We can tell how He loves us;

We can tell about Jesus,

And the great things God has done.

Action Option: Children demonstrate the sign for "Jesus."

Enrichment Option: Divide group—one group sings first half of first three lines ("We can tell") and other group sings rest of each line; all sing the last line.

"we can tell"

"great things"

"God has done"

*Words and Music by Marc and Judy Roth. © 2001 Gospel Light. Permission to photocopy granted. Shake It Up!*

# Go and Tell

## (Mark 16:15)

Words and Music by Mary Gross

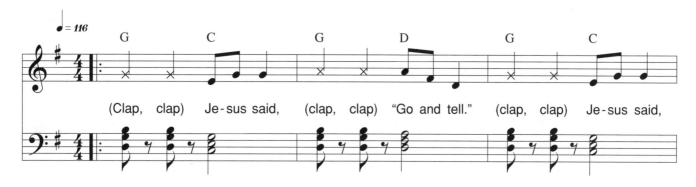

(Clap, clap) Je-sus said, (clap, clap) "Go and tell." (clap, clap) Je-sus said,

"Go and tell the good news." (Clap, clap) Je-sus said, (clap, clap) "Go and tell."

(clap, clap) Je-sus said, "Go and tell the good news."

# Go and Tell

**(Mark 16:15)**

(*Clap twice.*) Jesus said,

(*Clap twice.*) "Go and tell."

(*Clap twice.*) Jesus said,

"Go and tell the good news."
  (*Clap three times in rhythm
  while singing last line.*)


(*Clap twice.*) Jesus said,

(*Clap twice.*) "Go and tell."

(*Clap twice.*) Jesus said,

"Go and tell the good news."
  (*Clap three times in rhythm
  while singing last line.*)

***Repeat song***

Action Option: When song is repeated, stomp, pat knees
or touch shoulders instead of clapping.

# God Is with Me

Words and Music by Marc and Judy Roth

1. God is with me all the time, Name a time! (day - time)
2. God will help me share my cars, Name a time! (play - time)
3. God will help me do what's right Name a time! (bed - time)

God is with me all the time, ev - 'ry time___ of day.
God will help me share my cars, ev - 'ry time___ of day.
God will help me do what's right, ev - 'ry time___ of day,

Ev - 'ry time___ of day, Ev - 'ry time___ of day.

# God Is with Me

God is with me all the time.

Name a time!

*(Child responds by saying a time of day ["daytime," "bedtime," "snack time," "nap time," etc.].)*

God is with me all the time,
  every time of day.

"with"


God will help me share my <u>cars</u>.

Name a time!

*(Child responds by saying a time of day ["daytime," "bedtime," "snack time," "nap time," etc.].)*

God will help me share my <u>cars</u>,
  every time of day.

"every time"


God will help me do what's right.

Name a time!

*(Child responds by saying a time of day ["daytime," "bedtime," "snack time," "nap time," etc.].)*

God will help me do what's right,
  every time of day.

Every time of day, every time of day.

"help"

**Enrichment Option: Replace underlined words with children's ideas of other items to share.**

*Words and Music by Marc and Judy Roth. © 2001 Gospel Light. Permission to photocopy granted. Shake It Up!*

# God with You

## (Joshua 1:9)

Words and Music by Marc and Judy Roth

♩ = 110

F

(the Lord your God)

The Lord your God    Will be with

C    (will be with you)    (wher - ev - er you go),

you    Wher - ev - er you    go    Wher - ev - er you

F    (wher - ev - er you go).    (the Lord your God)

go    The Lord your    God    Will be with

C    (will be with you)    (wher - ev - er you go),

you    Wher - ev - er you    go    Wher - ev - er you

F    (wher - ev - er you go).    *Fine*

go    The Lord your God    will

# God with You

**(Joshua 1:9)**

*Chorus:*

**The Lord your God (the Lord your God)**

  *(Make big L with arms.)*

**Will be with you (will be with you)**

  *(Put fists together for "with.")*

**Wherever you go (wherever you go),**

  *(March in place.)*

**Wherever you go (wherever you go).**

  *(March in place.)*


*Repeat chorus*


The Lord your God will be with you

  wherever you go, wherever you go.

The Lord your God will be with you

  wherever you go, wherever you go.


*Chorus*

Words and Music by Marc and Judy Roth. © 2001 Gospel Light. Permission to photocopy granted. *Shake It Up!*

# God's Care

Words and Music by Mary Gross

1. When I'm hun-gry, I need food, food, food.
2. When I'm scared, I need to know, know, know

I'm so glad that God is good, good, good.
God's with me where-e'er I go, go, go.

When I ask Him, He will give, give, give
God will hear me when I pray, pray, pray;

Ev-'ry-thing I need to live, live, live!
He will help me ev-'ry day, day, day!

# God's Care

When I'm hungry, I need food,

food, food. *(Rub tummy.)*

I'm so glad that God is good,

good, good. *(Pat chest.)*

When I ask Him, He will give,

give, give *(Pretend to give.)*

Everything I need to live,

live, live! *(Clap three times.)*


When I'm scared, I need to know,

know, know *(Tap head.)*

God's with me wherever I go,

go, go. *(Pretend to walk.)*

God will hear me when I pray,

pray, pray; *(Pretend to pray.)*

He will help me every day,

day, day! *(Clap three times.)*

Words and Music by Mary Gross. © 2001 Gospel Light. Permission to photocopy granted. *Shake It Up!*

# Good to Me

## (Genesis 33:11)

Words and Music by Mary Gross

God has been good, good to me. God has been good,

good to me. God has been good,

good to me. God has been good to me.

**Spoken:**

*(Children perform actions as instructed.)*

**Line up and touch the shoulders of the person in front of you.**

**Let's walk while we sing!**

# Good to Me

**(Genesis 33:11)**

God has been good, good to me.

God has been good, good to me.

God has been good, good to me.

God has been good to me.

"good"
thumbs up sign

**Spoken:**

*(Children perform
actions as instructed.)*

**Line up and touch the shoulders
of the person in front of you.
Let's walk while we sing!**

God has been good, good to me.

God has been good, good to me.

God has been good, good to me.

God has been good to me.

"me"

Enrichment Option: Invite older children to snap fingers as they sing.
Younger children may point to themselves as they sing the words "good to me."

*Words and Music by Mary Gross. © 2001 Gospel Light. Permission to photocopy granted. Shake It Up!*

# Heroes

Words and Music by Mary Gross

# Heroes

God helped Joshua,

   God helped Deborah—

   *(Count on fingers.)*

They were heroes!

   God made them strong.

   *(Flex arms.)*

God helped Joash and Esther, too.

   *(Count on fingers.)*

God helps me and God helps you!

   *(Point for "me" and "you.")*

We can be heroes when we obey.

   *(Nod.)*

When we trust God and do what

   He says, *(Count on fingers.)*

God will teach us to act

   in good ways—*(Nod.)*

We can be heroes, too! *(Flex arms.)*

*Words and Music by Mary Gross. © 2001 Gospel Light. Permission to photocopy granted. Shake It Up!*

# My Helper

## (Hebrews 13:6)

Words and Music by Mary Gross

The Lord is my help-er;____ I will not be a - fraid.

The Lord is my help-er;____ The

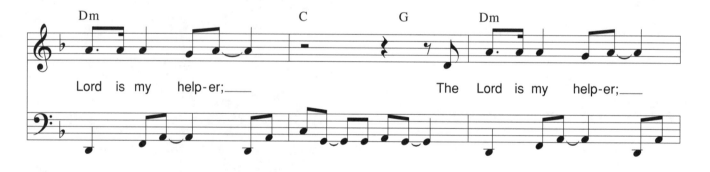

Lord is my help-er;____ The Lord is my help-er;____

I will not be a - fraid.

**Spoken:**

*(Teacher asks questions; children answer.)*

**Chin up? Chin up! Big smile? Big smile! Afraid? No way!**

# My Helper

(Hebrews 13:6)

*Chorus:*

**The Lord is my helper;**

**I will not be afraid.**

**The Lord is my helper;**

**I will not be afraid.**

The Lord is my helper!

The Lord is my helper!

The Lord is my helper!

I will not be afraid.

*Spoken:*

*(Teacher asks questions; children answer.)*

**Chin up? Chin up!**

**Big smile? Big smile!**

**Afraid? No way!**

"the Lord is my helper"

"I will not be afraid"

Action Option: Nod while singing "The Lord is my helper"; then shake head no while singing "I will not be afraid."

Words and Music by Mary Gross. © 2001 Gospel Light. Permission to photocopy granted. *Shake It Up!*

# Alphabetical Index

# Scripture Index

# Topical Index

## GOD'S GIFTS

## JESUS

## OUR BIBLE

## (continued)

## FRIENDS

## SEASONS

## PLEASING GOD

## PRAISING GOD

## FAMILY